DATE DUE			

164729

612.8
BEK

Bekkering, Annalise.

Sight

ALICE GUSTAFSON ELEMENTARY LRC

709205 01446   37167C   0001

Sight

Annalise Bekkering

Published by Weigl Publishers Inc.
350 5th Avenue, Suite 3304, PMB 6G
New York, NY 10118-0069
Website: www.weigl.com

Library of Congress Cataloging-in-Publication Data

Bekkering, Annalise.
 Sight / Annalise Bekkering.
    p. cm. -- (World of wonder)
 Includes index.
 ISBN 978-1-60596-052-4 (hard cover : alk. paper) -- ISBN 978-1-60596-053-1 (soft cover : alk. paper)
 1. Vision--Juvenile literature. 2. Eye--Juvenile literature. I. Title.
 QP475.7.B45 2010
 612.8'4--dc22
                              2009001959

Printed in China
1 2 3 4 5 6 7 8 9 0 13 12 11 10 09

Editor: Heather C. Hudak
Design and Layout: Terry Paulhus

Weigl acknowledges Getty Images as its primary image supplier for this title.

CONTENTS

What is Sight?

How do you know the color of a crayon or the shape of a fruit? Our eyes tell us. With our eyes, we can see everything from stars to sand grains.

Sight is one of our **senses**. It helps us learn about our surroundings.

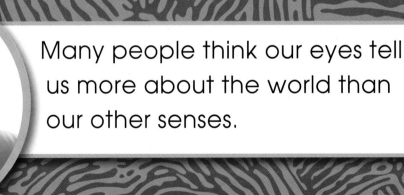

Many people think our eyes tell us more about the world than our other senses.

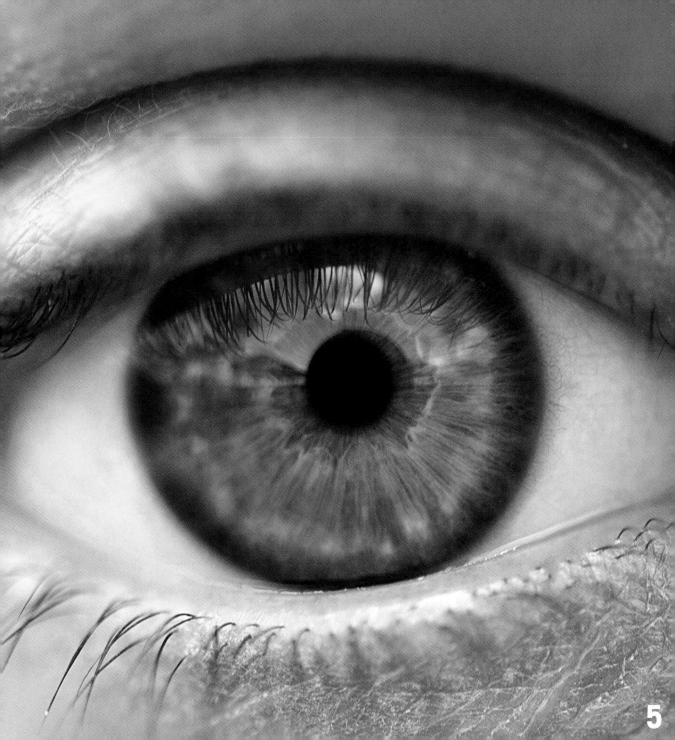

Let the Light Shine In

What can you see when you turn out the lights? You likely cannot see well. This is because we need light to see.

Light **reflects** off objects and enters our eyes. This is how we see the size, shape, color, and **texture** of an object, such as a building.

Light comes from many sources, including the Sun, a light bulb, or fire.

In Your Eyes

Did you know that your eyes work like a camera? They help our brains make a picture of the world.

Like a camera, each of our eyes has a lens. Tiny **muscles** squeeze and stretch the lenses. This makes blurry images sharp.

The colored part of our eyes is called the iris. It has a black dot in the center. This is the pupil. Light enters the eye through the pupil. The pupil can open up wide to let in more light. This helps us see better in the dark. The pupil narrows in bright light.

Spotty Vision

Close one eye, and look at the tip of a pencil. Slowly move the pencil closer. Can you always see the pencil tip?

A special kind of skin inside your eyes can sense light. One spot does not have this skin. It cannot sense light. This is called a **blind** spot.

Upside-down World

Did you know when a picture of an object enters our eyes, it is upside-down? You can see the same thing happen if you look at your reflection in a shiny spoon.

Our brain flips the image so it appears right-side-up when we see it.

Go Long

Do both of your eyes see exactly the same thing? Close one eye. As you open it, close the other eye. Did you notice that each eye sees a slightly different picture of the world?

With one eye closed, try to touch the tips of two fingers together. Open both eyes, and try to touch the tips together. Was it easier with both eyes open?

Seeing both pictures at once tells us how near or far an object is. This helps us do things such as walk, throw a ball, or pour juice.

Seeing is Believing

Is there a connection between what we see and how we feel? Colors can change a person's mood. Some people feel calm when they see blue. It may remind them of a clear sky. Yellow is a warning color in nature. Some insects with painful stings are yellow.

Look at the colors in the picture. How does each color make you feel?

ALICE GUSTAFSON
SCHOOL
LEARNING CENTER

Beastly Points of View

Did you know that many animals see the world differently than we do? Some do not see color very well. Others, such as cats, see better in the dark.

Snakes see body heat that comes from other animals. This heat makes a special kind of light that we cannot see.

Bees can also see a kind of light that we cannot. This light helps bees find flowers among other plants.

19

In Living Color

Did you know that one person in twelve has trouble seeing color? This is called color blindness. Color-blind people cannot see certain colors. Many see red and green as shades of yellow. Color-blindness is much more common in boys than in girls.

Can you see the number "5" in this circle? If not, you may be color blind.

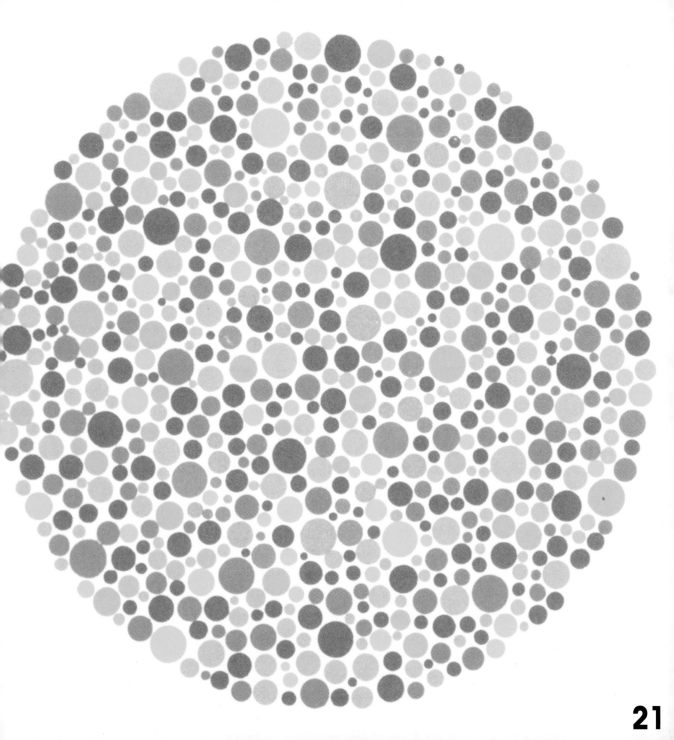

21

Test Your Sense of Sight

Supplies
a sheet of construction paper

1. Roll up the piece of construction paper into a tube.

2. Place the tube in your right hand. Hold up your left hand, and rest the end of the tube between your thumb and index finger.

3. Keep both eyes open, and look through the tube with your right eye. Do you see a hole through your hand? This happens because your brain gets different views from each eye.

Find Out More

To learn more about sight, visit these websites.

The SDC Colour Museum
www.colour-experience.
org/focus/colour_museum/
colour_museum1.htm

**National Institute of
Environmental Health
Sciences**
http://kids.niehs.nih.gov/
illusion/illusions.htm

Weather Wiz Kids
www.weatherwizkids.com/
optical_illusions.htm

BBC Science
www.bbc.co.uk/schools/
ks2bitesize/science/
activities/see_things.shtml

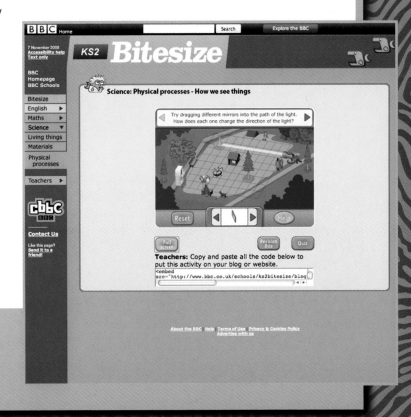

Glossary

blind: unable to see

muscles: parts of the body that pull against other parts of the body to move them

reflects: bounces back

senses: ways the body gets information about what is happening in its surroundings

texture: ways something feels to touch

Index

blind 10

color-blind 20

iris 8

lens 8

reflect 7, 13